Astronomy For Kids

Planets, Stars and Constellations

Intergalactic Kids Book Edition

SPEEDY
PUBLISHING

Speedy Publishing LLC
40 E. Main St. #1156
Newark, DE 19711
www.speedypublishing.com

PLANETS

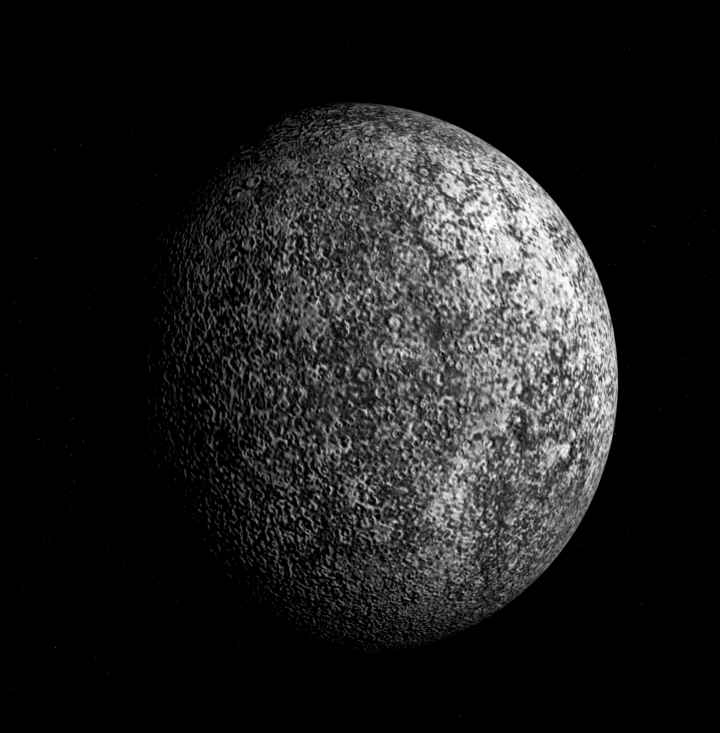

Mercury takes 59 days to make a rotation but only 88 days to circle the Sun.

Venus is the brightest planet in our sky and can sometimes be seen with the naked eye if you know where to look.

Earth has more exposed water than land. Three quarters of the Earth is covered by water!

Mars is the home of "Olympus Mons", the largest volcano found in the solar system.

Jupiter is the largest planet in the solar system, but it spins very quickly on its axis.

Saturn is the second biggest planet, but it's also the lightest planet.

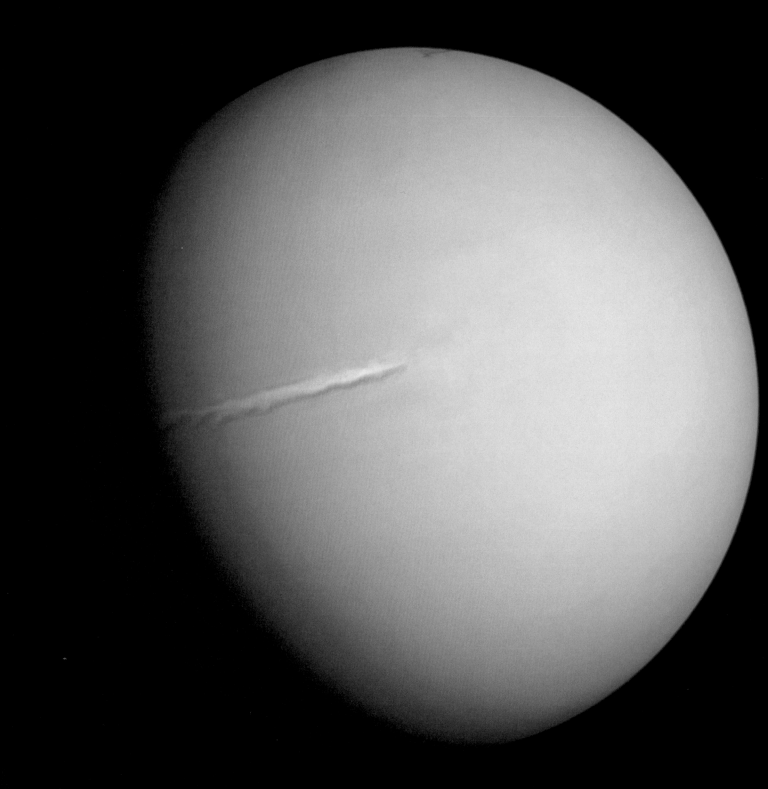

Uranus' axis is at
a 97 degree angle,
meaning that it orbits
lying on its side!

Neptune was discovered in 1846. In 2011 it finally made it's first lap around the sun because one Neptune year lasts 165 Earth years!

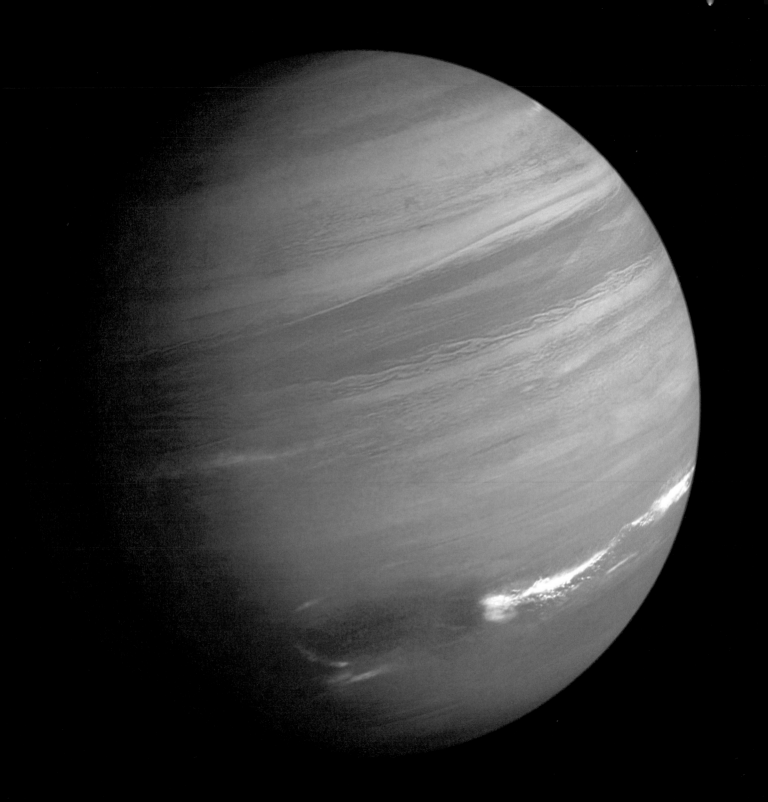

In 2006, Pluto is no longer considered a major planet, instead it is now a dwarf planet.

STARS &
CONSTELLATIONS

The star that is closest to the Earth is the sun.

A Star is a gigantic, glowing ball of plasma.

Most stars are between 1 billion and 10 billion years old.

The hottest stars give off a bluish light while the cooler stars give off a reddish light.

Stars seem to twinkle because their light travels through the earth's atmosphere and the turbulence in the atmosphere affects the way stars are seen.

Constellations are star patterns in the night sky.

There are 88 official constellations.

Different constellations become visible throughout the year